50 Nourishing Healthy Cooking Recipes

By: Kelly Johnson

Table of Contents

- Quinoa and Chickpea Salad
- Grilled Lemon Herb Salmon
- Avocado Toast with Poached Egg
- Zucchini Noodles with Pesto
- Baked Sweet Potato Fries
- Spaghetti Squash Primavera
- Cauliflower Rice Stir-Fry
- Chickpea and Spinach Curry
- Grilled Veggie Buddha Bowl
- Sweet Potato and Black Bean Tacos
- Almond-Crusted Chicken Tenders
- Lentil Soup with Kale
- Grilled Chicken Salad with Avocado
- Baked Cod with Asparagus
- Spicy Roasted Chickpeas
- Roasted Brussels Sprouts with Balsamic
- Cauliflower and Lentil Tacos

- Salmon and Avocado Sushi Rolls
- Miso Soup with Tofu and Seaweed
- Quinoa-Stuffed Bell Peppers
- Grilled Shrimp with Mango Salsa
- Mediterranean Hummus Bowl
- Roasted Butternut Squash Soup
- Avocado and Tomato Salad
- Grilled Chicken with Roasted Vegetables
- Vegan Buddha Bowl with Tahini Dressing
- Spinach and Mushroom Frittata
- Baked Chicken with Sweet Potato Mash
- Beetroot Salad with Goat Cheese
- Thai Peanut Chicken Lettuce Wraps
- Almond Butter and Banana Smoothie
- Spicy Roasted Cauliflower
- Black Bean and Quinoa Salad
- Turmeric Roasted Carrots
- Cucumber and Feta Salad
- Grilled Salmon with Avocado Salsa

- Sweet Potato and Kale Salad
- Coconut Curry Lentils
- Roasted Eggplant with Tahini Sauce
- Cabbage Stir-Fry with Tofu
- Avocado and Cucumber Sushi Rolls
- Chicken and Broccoli Stir-Fry
- Pesto Zoodles with Cherry Tomatoes
- Baked Falafel with Tahini
- Green Smoothie Bowl with Chia Seeds
- Roasted Vegetables with Quinoa
- Chickpea Salad with Cucumber and Dill
- Grilled Portobello Mushrooms with Garlic
- Salmon and Avocado Salad
- Cauliflower Pizza Crust with Veggies

Quinoa and Chickpea Salad

Ingredients:

- 1 cup quinoa, cooked
- 1 can chickpeas, drained and rinsed
- 1 cucumber, diced
- 1 red bell pepper, diced
- 1/4 red onion, finely chopped
- 1/4 cup fresh parsley, chopped
- 1/4 cup feta cheese (optional)
- 2 tbsp olive oil
- 1 tbsp lemon juice
- Salt and pepper to taste

Instructions:

1. In a large bowl, combine the cooked quinoa, chickpeas, cucumber, red bell pepper, red onion, and parsley.
2. Drizzle with olive oil and lemon juice. Toss until everything is evenly coated.
3. Season with salt and pepper to taste.
4. Top with feta cheese if desired, and serve chilled or at room temperature.

Grilled Lemon Herb Salmon

Ingredients:

- 4 salmon fillets
- 2 tbsp olive oil
- 1 lemon, sliced
- 2 garlic cloves, minced
- 1 tbsp fresh parsley, chopped
- 1 tbsp fresh thyme
- Salt and pepper to taste

Instructions:

1. Preheat the grill to medium heat.
2. In a small bowl, mix olive oil, garlic, parsley, thyme, lemon juice, salt, and pepper.
3. Brush the salmon fillets with the herb mixture and place the lemon slices on top.
4. Grill the salmon for 4-5 minutes on each side until cooked through and flaky.
5. Serve with a side of roasted veggies or a salad.

Avocado Toast with Poached Egg

Ingredients:

- 2 slices whole grain bread, toasted
- 1 ripe avocado
- 2 eggs
- 1 tbsp white vinegar
- Salt and pepper to taste
- Red pepper flakes (optional)

Instructions:

1. Mash the avocado in a bowl and season with salt and pepper.
2. In a small pot, bring water to a simmer and add the vinegar. Gently crack the eggs into the simmering water and poach for about 3-4 minutes until the whites are set and the yolks are runny.
3. Spread the mashed avocado evenly onto the toasted bread.
4. Carefully place a poached egg on top of each slice of avocado toast.
5. Sprinkle with red pepper flakes if desired, and serve immediately.

Zucchini Noodles with Pesto

Ingredients:

- 4 medium zucchinis, spiralized into noodles
- 1 cup basil pesto (store-bought or homemade)
- 1 tbsp olive oil
- 1/4 cup pine nuts, toasted (optional)
- Fresh parmesan cheese for garnish

Instructions:

1. Heat the olive oil in a large skillet over medium heat.
2. Add the zucchini noodles and cook for 2-3 minutes, stirring occasionally, until they are just tender.
3. Remove the skillet from the heat and toss the zucchini noodles with the pesto until well coated.
4. Garnish with toasted pine nuts and fresh parmesan cheese.
5. Serve immediately, and enjoy a low-carb, flavorful meal!

Baked Sweet Potato Fries

Ingredients:

- 2 medium sweet potatoes, peeled and cut into fries
- 2 tbsp olive oil
- 1 tsp paprika
- 1/2 tsp garlic powder
- 1/4 tsp cayenne pepper (optional)
- Salt and pepper to taste

Instructions:

1. Preheat the oven to 425°F (220°C).
2. Toss the sweet potato fries with olive oil, paprika, garlic powder, cayenne pepper, salt, and pepper.
3. Spread the fries in a single layer on a baking sheet.
4. Bake for 25-30 minutes, flipping halfway through, until crispy and golden brown.
5. Serve with your favorite dipping sauce.

Spaghetti Squash Primavera

Ingredients:

- 1 medium spaghetti squash
- 1 tbsp olive oil
- 1 cup cherry tomatoes, halved
- 1 bell pepper, diced
- 1 zucchini, sliced
- 1/2 red onion, thinly sliced
- 2 garlic cloves, minced
- 1/4 cup fresh basil, chopped
- Salt and pepper to taste
- Grated parmesan cheese for topping

Instructions:

1. Preheat the oven to 400°F (200°C).

2. Cut the spaghetti squash in half lengthwise, scoop out the seeds, and drizzle with olive oil. Season with salt and pepper.

3. Place the squash halves on a baking sheet, cut side down, and roast for 30-35 minutes until tender.

4. While the squash roasts, heat olive oil in a large pan and sauté the garlic, cherry tomatoes, bell pepper, zucchini, and onion until tender, about 5-7 minutes.

5. Once the squash is done, scrape out the flesh with a fork to create spaghetti-like strands.

6. Toss the squash strands with the sautéed vegetables and fresh basil.

7. Serve with grated parmesan on top.

Cauliflower Rice Stir-Fry

Ingredients:

- 1 head cauliflower, grated or processed into rice-sized pieces
- 2 tbsp olive oil
- 1/2 onion, diced
- 2 garlic cloves, minced
- 1 cup mixed veggies (carrots, peas, bell peppers)
- 2 eggs, lightly beaten
- 2 tbsp soy sauce or coconut aminos
- Salt and pepper to taste
- Green onions for garnish

Instructions:

1. Heat olive oil in a large skillet or wok over medium heat.
2. Add the onion and garlic and sauté for 2-3 minutes until fragrant.
3. Add the mixed veggies and cook for 3-5 minutes until tender.
4. Push the veggies to one side of the pan and pour the beaten eggs on the other side. Scramble the eggs until cooked through.
5. Add the cauliflower rice to the pan, stir to combine, and cook for 5-7 minutes, stirring occasionally, until tender.
6. Drizzle with soy sauce and season with salt and pepper.

7. Garnish with green onions and serve.

Chickpea and Spinach Curry

Ingredients:

- 1 can chickpeas, drained and rinsed
- 2 cups fresh spinach
- 1 onion, diced
- 2 garlic cloves, minced
- 1 tbsp grated ginger
- 1 tbsp curry powder
- 1/2 tsp turmeric
- 1/2 cup coconut milk
- 1 can diced tomatoes
- 2 tbsp olive oil
- Salt and pepper to taste

Instructions:

1. Heat olive oil in a large pot over medium heat. Add the onion and garlic and sauté for 2-3 minutes.

2. Add the ginger, curry powder, and turmeric, and cook for 1 more minute.

3. Stir in the coconut milk and diced tomatoes. Bring to a simmer.

4. Add the chickpeas and spinach, and cook for 5-7 minutes until the spinach is wilted and the chickpeas are heated through.

5. Season with salt and pepper to taste and serve with rice or naan.

Grilled Veggie Buddha Bowl

Ingredients:

- 1 cup quinoa, cooked
- 1 cup mixed veggies (bell peppers, zucchini, mushrooms, carrots), sliced
- 1 tbsp olive oil
- 1 tbsp balsamic vinegar
- 1 tbsp lemon juice
- 1 tbsp tahini
- Salt and pepper to taste
- Fresh parsley for garnish

Instructions:

1. Preheat the grill or grill pan to medium-high heat.
2. Toss the mixed veggies with olive oil, balsamic vinegar, salt, and pepper.
3. Grill the veggies for 5-7 minutes, turning occasionally until tender and charred.
4. To assemble the bowl, place the cooked quinoa at the base, then top with the grilled veggies.
5. Drizzle with tahini, lemon juice, and fresh parsley.

Sweet Potato and Black Bean Tacos

Ingredients:

- 2 medium sweet potatoes, peeled and diced
- 1 can black beans, drained and rinsed
- 1 tbsp olive oil
- 1 tsp cumin
- 1/2 tsp paprika
- Salt and pepper to taste
- 8 small corn tortillas
- Toppings: avocado, cilantro, lime wedges, salsa

Instructions:

1. Preheat the oven to 400°F (200°C).
2. Toss the diced sweet potatoes with olive oil, cumin, paprika, salt, and pepper. Spread on a baking sheet and roast for 25-30 minutes, flipping halfway through.
3. Warm the tortillas in a skillet or oven.
4. Once the sweet potatoes are roasted, assemble the tacos by placing a few spoonfuls of sweet potatoes and black beans in each tortilla.
5. Top with avocado, cilantro, lime juice, and salsa.

Almond-Crusted Chicken Tenders

Ingredients:

- 4 chicken tenders
- 1/2 cup almond flour
- 1 egg, beaten
- 1/4 cup grated parmesan cheese
- 1/2 tsp garlic powder
- Salt and pepper to taste
- 2 tbsp olive oil

Instructions:

1. Preheat the oven to 400°F (200°C).
2. In a shallow dish, combine almond flour, parmesan cheese, garlic powder, salt, and pepper.
3. Dip each chicken tender into the beaten egg, then coat in the almond flour mixture.
4. Heat olive oil in a skillet over medium heat. Cook the chicken tenders for 2-3 minutes on each side until golden brown.
5. Transfer the chicken to a baking sheet and bake for 10-12 minutes until fully cooked through.

Lentil Soup with Kale

Ingredients:

- 1 cup lentils, rinsed
- 1 bunch kale, chopped
- 1 onion, diced
- 2 garlic cloves, minced
- 2 carrots, diced
- 1 celery stalk, diced
- 1 can diced tomatoes
- 4 cups vegetable broth
- 1 tbsp olive oil
- 1 tsp thyme
- Salt and pepper to taste

Instructions:

1. Heat olive oil in a large pot over medium heat. Add the onion, garlic, carrots, and celery, and sauté for 5-7 minutes until softened.
2. Stir in the thyme, lentils, diced tomatoes, and vegetable broth. Bring to a boil.
3. Reduce heat and simmer for 30-35 minutes until the lentils are tender.
4. Add the kale and cook for an additional 5-7 minutes until the kale is wilted.
5. Season with salt and pepper, and serve warm.

Grilled Chicken Salad with Avocado

Ingredients:

- 2 chicken breasts
- 2 tbsp olive oil
- 1 tsp paprika
- 1 tsp garlic powder
- Salt and pepper to taste
- 1 avocado, sliced
- Mixed greens
- 1/2 cucumber, sliced
- 1/4 red onion, thinly sliced
- Dressing of your choice (vinaigrette, ranch, etc.)

Instructions:

1. Preheat the grill to medium-high heat.
2. Rub the chicken breasts with olive oil, paprika, garlic powder, salt, and pepper.
3. Grill the chicken for 6-7 minutes on each side until fully cooked.
4. Slice the chicken and arrange it on top of mixed greens, avocado, cucumber, and red onion.
5. Drizzle with your favorite dressing and serve.

Roasted Brussels Sprouts with Balsamic

Ingredients:

- 1 lb Brussels sprouts, trimmed and halved
- 2 tbsp olive oil
- 2 tbsp balsamic vinegar
- 1 tbsp honey or maple syrup
- Salt and pepper to taste

Instructions:

1. Preheat the oven to 400°F (200°C).
2. Toss the Brussels sprouts with olive oil, balsamic vinegar, honey, salt, and pepper.
3. Spread the Brussels sprouts on a baking sheet in a single layer.
4. Roast for 20-25 minutes, stirring halfway through, until they are golden and crispy.
5. Serve as a side dish or top with extra balsamic vinegar if desired.

Cauliflower and Lentil Tacos

Ingredients:

- 1 small cauliflower, cut into florets
- 1 cup cooked lentils
- 1 tbsp olive oil
- 1 tsp cumin
- 1 tsp paprika
- Salt and pepper to taste
- 8 small corn tortillas
- Toppings: avocado, cilantro, lime wedges, salsa

Instructions:

1. Preheat the oven to 400°F (200°C).
2. Toss the cauliflower florets with olive oil, cumin, paprika, salt, and pepper. Roast on a baking sheet for 20-25 minutes until tender.
3. Warm the tortillas in a skillet or oven.
4. To assemble the tacos, place the roasted cauliflower and lentils in each tortilla.
5. Top with avocado, cilantro, lime juice, and salsa.

Salmon and Avocado Sushi Rolls

Ingredients:

- 1 cup sushi rice, cooked and seasoned
- 4 sheets nori (seaweed)
- 1/2 lb fresh salmon, thinly sliced
- 1 avocado, thinly sliced
- Soy sauce for dipping

Instructions:

1. Place a sheet of nori on a bamboo sushi mat.
2. Spread a thin layer of sushi rice over the nori, leaving a 1-inch border at the top.
3. Lay the salmon and avocado slices along the bottom edge of the rice.
4. Roll the sushi tightly using the mat, then slice into 6-8 pieces.
5. Serve with soy sauce for dipping.

Miso Soup with Tofu and Seaweed

Ingredients:

- 4 cups vegetable broth
- 1/4 cup miso paste
- 1/2 cup cubed tofu
- 1/4 cup dried seaweed (wakame)
- 2 green onions, sliced
- 1 tbsp soy sauce (optional)

Instructions:

1. In a pot, heat the vegetable broth over medium heat.
2. Stir in the miso paste until dissolved.
3. Add the tofu, seaweed, and soy sauce (if using). Simmer for 5-7 minutes.
4. Garnish with sliced green onions and serve.

Quinoa-Stuffed Bell Peppers

Ingredients:

- 4 bell peppers, tops cut off and seeds removed
- 1 cup quinoa, cooked
- 1 can black beans, drained and rinsed
- 1 cup corn kernels
- 1 tsp cumin
- 1 tsp chili powder
- 1/2 cup shredded cheese (optional)
- Salt and pepper to taste

Instructions:

1. Preheat the oven to 375°F (190°C).
2. In a bowl, mix the cooked quinoa, black beans, corn, cumin, chili powder, salt, and pepper.
3. Stuff the mixture into each bell pepper.
4. Place the stuffed peppers in a baking dish and cover with foil. Bake for 25 minutes.
5. If desired, sprinkle with cheese and bake for an additional 5 minutes until melted.

Grilled Shrimp with Mango Salsa

Ingredients:

- 1 lb shrimp, peeled and deveined
- 1 tbsp olive oil
- 1 tbsp lime juice
- 1 tsp cumin
- Salt and pepper to taste
- 1 mango, diced
- 1/4 red onion, diced
- 1/4 cup cilantro, chopped
- 1 tbsp lime juice

Instructions:

1. Preheat the grill to medium-high heat.
2. Toss the shrimp with olive oil, lime juice, cumin, salt, and pepper.
3. Grill the shrimp for 2-3 minutes on each side until pink and cooked through.
4. In a bowl, combine the diced mango, red onion, cilantro, and lime juice to make the salsa.
5. Serve the shrimp with a generous spoonful of mango salsa on top.

Mediterranean Hummus Bowl

Ingredients:

- 1 cup hummus
- 1 cup cherry tomatoes, halved
- 1 cucumber, diced
- 1/4 red onion, thinly sliced
- 1/4 cup Kalamata olives, pitted and chopped
- 1/4 cup feta cheese, crumbled
- Fresh parsley for garnish

Instructions:

1. Spread the hummus in a bowl or on a plate.
2. Top with cherry tomatoes, cucumber, red onion, olives, feta cheese, and parsley.
3. Serve with pita bread or fresh vegetables for dipping.

Roasted Butternut Squash Soup

Ingredients:

- 1 medium butternut squash, peeled, seeded, and cubed
- 1 onion, diced
- 2 garlic cloves, minced
- 4 cups vegetable broth
- 1 tsp ground ginger
- Salt and pepper to taste
- 1/4 cup coconut milk (optional)

Instructions:

1. Preheat the oven to 400°F (200°C).
2. Toss the cubed butternut squash with olive oil, salt, and pepper, and roast for 25-30 minutes until tender.
3. In a large pot, sauté the onion and garlic until softened.
4. Add the roasted squash, vegetable broth, ginger, salt, and pepper. Bring to a boil.
5. Simmer for 10 minutes, then blend the soup until smooth using an immersion blender or regular blender.
6. Stir in coconut milk if using, and serve.

Avocado and Tomato Salad

Ingredients:

- 2 avocados, diced
- 1 pint cherry tomatoes, halved
- 1/4 red onion, thinly sliced
- 1/4 cup fresh basil, chopped
- 1 tbsp olive oil
- 1 tbsp balsamic vinegar
- Salt and pepper to taste

Instructions:

1. In a bowl, combine the avocado, cherry tomatoes, red onion, and basil.
2. Drizzle with olive oil and balsamic vinegar, and season with salt and pepper.
3. Toss gently and serve immediately.

Grilled Chicken with Roasted Vegetables

Ingredients:

- 2 chicken breasts
- 1 tbsp olive oil
- 1 tsp paprika
- 1 tsp garlic powder
- Salt and pepper to taste
- 2 cups mixed vegetables (carrots, zucchini, bell peppers, etc.)

Instructions:

1. Preheat the grill to medium-high heat.
2. Rub the chicken breasts with olive oil, paprika, garlic powder, salt, and pepper.
3. Grill the chicken for 6-7 minutes on each side until fully cooked.
4. Meanwhile, toss the mixed vegetables with olive oil, salt, and pepper, and roast them in the oven at 400°F (200°C) for 20 minutes.
5. Serve the grilled chicken with the roasted vegetables.

Vegan Buddha Bowl with Tahini Dressing

Ingredients:

- 1 cup cooked quinoa
- 1 cup roasted chickpeas
- 1/2 avocado, sliced
- 1/2 cup shredded carrots
- 1/2 cup steamed broccoli
- 1/4 cup red cabbage, thinly sliced
- 2 tbsp tahini
- 1 tbsp lemon juice
- 1 tbsp water
- Salt and pepper to taste

Instructions:

1. Prepare all the ingredients: cook the quinoa, roast chickpeas, steam the broccoli, and slice the vegetables.

2. In a small bowl, mix the tahini, lemon juice, water, salt, and pepper to make the dressing.

3. In a large bowl or plate, layer the quinoa, chickpeas, avocado, shredded carrots, broccoli, and red cabbage.

4. Drizzle the tahini dressing on top and enjoy!

Spinach and Mushroom Frittata

Ingredients:

- 6 large eggs
- 1 cup spinach, chopped
- 1/2 cup mushrooms, sliced
- 1/4 cup feta cheese, crumbled (optional)
- 1/4 cup milk (or non-dairy alternative)
- 1 tbsp olive oil
- Salt and pepper to taste

Instructions:

1. Preheat the oven to 375°F (190°C).
2. In a skillet, heat the olive oil over medium heat and sauté the mushrooms until soft.
3. Add the spinach and cook until wilted.
4. In a bowl, whisk together the eggs, milk, salt, and pepper.
5. Pour the egg mixture into the skillet and cook for 2-3 minutes until the edges begin to set.
6. Transfer the skillet to the oven and bake for 10-12 minutes or until fully set.
7. Remove from the oven and sprinkle with feta cheese (if using) before serving.

Baked Chicken with Sweet Potato Mash

Ingredients:

- 2 chicken breasts
- 2 medium sweet potatoes, peeled and cubed
- 1 tbsp olive oil
- 1 tsp paprika
- 1 tsp garlic powder
- Salt and pepper to taste

Instructions:

1. Preheat the oven to 400°F (200°C).
2. Rub the chicken breasts with olive oil, paprika, garlic powder, salt, and pepper.
3. Place the chicken breasts on a baking sheet and bake for 20-25 minutes, until fully cooked.
4. While the chicken bakes, boil the sweet potatoes in a pot of water until tender, about 15 minutes.
5. Mash the sweet potatoes with a fork or potato masher, and season with salt and pepper to taste.
6. Serve the baked chicken with the sweet potato mash.

Beetroot Salad with Goat Cheese

Ingredients:

- 2 medium beets, roasted and peeled
- 1/4 cup goat cheese, crumbled
- 1/4 cup walnuts, chopped
- 1 tbsp balsamic vinegar
- 2 tbsp olive oil
- Salt and pepper to taste

Instructions:

1. Preheat the oven to 400°F (200°C). Wrap the beets in foil and roast for 45-60 minutes until tender.
2. Let the beets cool, then peel and slice them.
3. In a bowl, combine the roasted beet slices, goat cheese, and walnuts.
4. Drizzle with balsamic vinegar and olive oil, and season with salt and pepper.
5. Toss gently and serve.

Thai Peanut Chicken Lettuce Wraps

Ingredients:

- 2 chicken breasts, cooked and shredded
- 1/4 cup peanut butter
- 2 tbsp soy sauce
- 1 tbsp lime juice
- 1 tsp grated ginger
- 1/4 cup chopped cilantro
- 1/4 cup shredded carrots
- 1 head of butter lettuce, separated into leaves

Instructions:

1. In a bowl, whisk together the peanut butter, soy sauce, lime juice, and grated ginger to make the peanut sauce.
2. Add the shredded chicken to the sauce and mix well.
3. Assemble the wraps by placing a spoonful of the chicken mixture in a lettuce leaf.
4. Top with chopped cilantro and shredded carrots.
5. Roll up and serve.

Almond Butter and Banana Smoothie

Ingredients:

- 1 banana
- 1 tbsp almond butter
- 1/2 cup almond milk (or non-dairy alternative)
- 1/2 cup ice
- 1 tsp honey (optional)

Instructions:

1. Place the banana, almond butter, almond milk, ice, and honey (if using) in a blender.
2. Blend until smooth and creamy.
3. Pour into a glass and enjoy!

Spicy Roasted Cauliflower

Ingredients:

- 1 medium cauliflower, cut into florets
- 2 tbsp olive oil
- 1 tsp chili powder
- 1/2 tsp paprika
- 1/2 tsp garlic powder
- Salt and pepper to taste

Instructions:

1. Preheat the oven to 425°F (220°C).
2. Toss the cauliflower florets with olive oil, chili powder, paprika, garlic powder, salt, and pepper.
3. Spread the cauliflower on a baking sheet in a single layer.
4. Roast for 20-25 minutes, until golden and crispy.
5. Serve as a side dish or snack.

Black Bean and Quinoa Salad

Ingredients:

- 1 cup cooked quinoa
- 1 can black beans, drained and rinsed
- 1 cup corn kernels
- 1/2 red bell pepper, diced
- 1/4 cup cilantro, chopped
- 1 tbsp lime juice
- 1 tbsp olive oil
- Salt and pepper to taste

Instructions:

1. In a bowl, combine the cooked quinoa, black beans, corn, red bell pepper, and cilantro.
2. Drizzle with lime juice and olive oil, and season with salt and pepper.
3. Toss to combine and serve.

Turmeric Roasted Carrots

Ingredients:

- 4-5 medium carrots, peeled and sliced
- 1 tbsp olive oil
- 1/2 tsp ground turmeric
- 1/2 tsp ground cumin
- Salt and pepper to taste

Instructions:

1. Preheat the oven to 400°F (200°C).
2. Toss the sliced carrots with olive oil, turmeric, cumin, salt, and pepper.
3. Spread the carrots on a baking sheet and roast for 20-25 minutes, until tender.
4. Serve as a side dish.

Cucumber and Feta Salad

Ingredients:

- 1 cucumber, thinly sliced
- 1/4 cup feta cheese, crumbled
- 1/4 red onion, thinly sliced
- 1 tbsp olive oil
- 1 tbsp red wine vinegar
- Salt and pepper to taste

Instructions:

1. In a bowl, combine the cucumber, feta cheese, and red onion.
2. Drizzle with olive oil and red wine vinegar.
3. Season with salt and pepper and toss gently.
4. Serve as a refreshing side salad.

Grilled Salmon with Avocado Salsa

Ingredients:

- 2 salmon fillets
- 1 tbsp olive oil
- 1 tbsp lemon juice
- 1 avocado, diced
- 1/2 cup cherry tomatoes, halved
- 1/4 cup red onion, diced
- 1 tbsp cilantro, chopped
- Salt and pepper to taste

Instructions:

1. Preheat the grill to medium-high heat.
2. Rub the salmon fillets with olive oil, lemon juice, salt, and pepper.
3. Grill the salmon for 4-5 minutes on each side, until cooked through.
4. In a bowl, combine the diced avocado, cherry tomatoes, red onion, and cilantro to make the salsa.
5. Serve the grilled salmon with the avocado salsa on top.

Sweet Potato and Kale Salad

Ingredients:

- 1 large sweet potato, peeled and diced
- 2 cups kale, chopped
- 1/4 cup red onion, thinly sliced
- 1/4 cup cranberries (dried)
- 1/4 cup pumpkin seeds
- 1 tbsp olive oil
- 1 tbsp balsamic vinegar
- 1 tsp honey (optional)
- Salt and pepper to taste

Instructions:

1. Preheat the oven to 400°F (200°C). Toss the sweet potato cubes with olive oil, salt, and pepper. Roast for 25-30 minutes, until tender.
2. Massage the kale with a little olive oil and salt to soften it.
3. In a large bowl, combine the roasted sweet potato, kale, red onion, cranberries, and pumpkin seeds.
4. In a small bowl, whisk together balsamic vinegar, honey (if using), salt, and pepper.
5. Drizzle the dressing over the salad and toss to combine. Serve immediately.

Coconut Curry Lentils

Ingredients:

- 1 cup red lentils, rinsed
- 1 can (13.5 oz) coconut milk
- 1 cup vegetable broth
- 1 onion, diced
- 2 garlic cloves, minced
- 1 tbsp curry powder
- 1/2 tsp ground turmeric
- 1/2 tsp cumin
- Salt and pepper to taste
- Fresh cilantro, for garnish

Instructions:

1. In a pot, heat some oil over medium heat and sauté the onion and garlic until softened.
2. Add the curry powder, turmeric, cumin, salt, and pepper, and cook for 1-2 minutes until fragrant.
3. Stir in the lentils, coconut milk, and vegetable broth. Bring to a boil, then reduce heat and simmer for 20-25 minutes, until the lentils are tender and the sauce has thickened.
4. Garnish with fresh cilantro and serve with rice or naan.

Roasted Eggplant with Tahini Sauce

Ingredients:

- 2 medium eggplants, sliced into rounds
- 2 tbsp olive oil
- Salt and pepper to taste
- 1/4 cup tahini
- 1 tbsp lemon juice
- 1 tbsp water (to thin the sauce)
- 1 garlic clove, minced
- Fresh parsley, chopped (for garnish)

Instructions:

1. Preheat the oven to 425°F (220°C). Place the eggplant slices on a baking sheet and drizzle with olive oil, salt, and pepper.
2. Roast for 20-25 minutes, flipping halfway through, until tender and golden brown.
3. In a small bowl, whisk together the tahini, lemon juice, water, garlic, salt, and pepper until smooth.
4. Drizzle the tahini sauce over the roasted eggplant slices and garnish with fresh parsley. Serve warm.

Cabbage Stir-Fry with Tofu

Ingredients:

- 1 block firm tofu, pressed and cubed
- 2 cups cabbage, shredded
- 1 carrot, julienned
- 2 tbsp soy sauce
- 1 tbsp sesame oil
- 1 tsp grated ginger
- 1 tbsp rice vinegar
- 1 tbsp sesame seeds (optional)
- Green onions, sliced (for garnish)

Instructions:

1. In a pan, heat the sesame oil over medium heat. Add the tofu cubes and cook until crispy and golden brown, about 5-7 minutes. Remove and set aside.
2. In the same pan, add the cabbage and carrot. Stir-fry for 5-7 minutes, until the cabbage is tender.
3. Add the soy sauce, rice vinegar, ginger, and tofu back into the pan. Stir to combine and cook for another 2-3 minutes.
4. Garnish with sesame seeds and green onions. Serve warm.

Avocado and Cucumber Sushi Rolls

Ingredients:

- 1 cup sushi rice, cooked
- 1 tbsp rice vinegar
- 1/2 tsp sugar
- 1/4 tsp salt
- 1/2 avocado, sliced thinly
- 1/2 cucumber, julienned
- 4 sheets nori (seaweed)
- Soy sauce for dipping

Instructions:

1. In a small bowl, combine the rice vinegar, sugar, and salt. Stir until dissolved. Mix into the cooked sushi rice.
2. Place a sheet of nori on a bamboo sushi mat. Spread a thin layer of rice over the nori, leaving about 1 inch at the top free.
3. Lay slices of avocado and cucumber in the center of the rice.
4. Roll the sushi tightly using the mat, sealing the edge with a little water.
5. Slice the roll into 6-8 pieces and serve with soy sauce for dipping.

Chicken and Broccoli Stir-Fry

Ingredients:

- 2 chicken breasts, thinly sliced
- 2 cups broccoli florets
- 1/4 cup soy sauce
- 1 tbsp sesame oil
- 1 tbsp honey
- 1 garlic clove, minced
- 1 tbsp grated ginger
- 2 tbsp rice vinegar
- 1 tsp cornstarch (optional, for thickening)
- Sesame seeds for garnish (optional)

Instructions:

1. Heat sesame oil in a pan over medium-high heat. Add the chicken slices and cook until browned and cooked through. Remove and set aside.
2. In the same pan, add the garlic and ginger and sauté for 1 minute.
3. Add the broccoli, soy sauce, honey, and rice vinegar. Stir to combine and cook until the broccoli is tender, about 5-7 minutes.
4. Return the chicken to the pan and stir to combine. If you want a thicker sauce, mix cornstarch with a little water and add it to the pan, stirring until the sauce thickens.

5. Garnish with sesame seeds and serve hot.

Pesto Zoodles with Cherry Tomatoes

Ingredients:

- 2 zucchinis, spiralized into noodles (zoodles)
- 1/2 cup cherry tomatoes, halved
- 2 tbsp pesto (store-bought or homemade)
- 1 tbsp olive oil
- Salt and pepper to taste

Instructions:

1. In a pan, heat the olive oil over medium heat. Add the zoodles and sauté for 2-3 minutes until tender.
2. Add the cherry tomatoes and pesto to the pan and stir to combine. Cook for another 2-3 minutes.
3. Season with salt and pepper to taste. Serve warm as a light and fresh meal.

Baked Falafel with Tahini

- Ingredients:

    1. 1 can (15 oz) chickpeas, drained and rinsed
    2. 1 small onion, chopped
    3. 2-3 cloves garlic, minced
    4. 1/4 cup fresh parsley, chopped
    5. 1/4 cup fresh cilantro, chopped
    6. 1 tbsp ground cumin
    7. 1 tbsp ground coriander
    8. 1/2 tsp ground turmeric
    9. Salt and pepper to taste
    10. 2-3 tbsp flour (chickpea or all-purpose)
    11. 1-2 tbsp olive oil
    12. 1 tbsp lemon juice

- Instructions:

    1. Preheat the oven to 375°F (190°C).
    2. In a food processor, blend chickpeas, onion, garlic, parsley, cilantro, cumin, coriander, turmeric, salt, and pepper until finely chopped but not pureed.
    3. Add flour and lemon juice, and pulse until combined. Add olive oil to help bind the mixture.

4. Shape into small balls or patties.

5. Place on a parchment-lined baking sheet and bake for 25-30 minutes, flipping halfway through, until golden brown.

6. Serve with tahini sauce on the side.

Green Smoothie Bowl with Chia Seeds

- Ingredients:

    1. 1 frozen banana
    2. 1/2 cup spinach or kale
    3. 1/2 cup almond milk (or any milk of choice)
    4. 1 tbsp chia seeds
    5. 1 tbsp honey or maple syrup (optional)
    6. Toppings: granola, fresh fruit, coconut flakes, nuts, seeds

- Instructions:

    1. Blend frozen banana, spinach, almond milk, chia seeds, and sweetener (if using) in a blender until smooth.
    2. Pour into a bowl and add toppings as desired.

Roasted Vegetables with Quinoa

- Ingredients:

    1. 2 cups mixed vegetables (carrots, bell peppers, zucchini, cauliflower, etc.)
    2. 1 tbsp olive oil
    3. Salt and pepper to taste
    4. 1 tsp dried herbs (thyme, rosemary, oregano)
    5. 1 cup quinoa
    6. 2 cups water or vegetable broth

- Instructions:

    1. Preheat the oven to 400°F (200°C).
    2. Toss the vegetables in olive oil, salt, pepper, and herbs. Spread them on a baking sheet and roast for 25-30 minutes until tender and slightly browned.
    3. Meanwhile, rinse the quinoa under cold water. Combine with water or broth in a pot, bring to a boil, then reduce to a simmer and cook for about 15 minutes, until the quinoa is cooked and fluffy.
    4. Serve roasted vegetables on top of the quinoa.

Chickpea Salad with Cucumber and Dill

- Ingredients:

    1. 1 can (15 oz) chickpeas, drained and rinsed
    2. 1 cucumber, diced
    3. 1/4 red onion, finely chopped
    4. 1 tbsp fresh dill, chopped
    5. 1 tbsp olive oil
    6. 1 tbsp lemon juice
    7. Salt and pepper to taste

- Instructions:

    1. In a bowl, combine chickpeas, cucumber, onion, and dill.
    2. Drizzle with olive oil and lemon juice, season with salt and pepper, and toss to combine.
    3. Serve immediately or chill for a few hours to allow flavors to meld.

Grilled Portobello Mushrooms with Garlic

- Ingredients:

    1. 4 large Portobello mushrooms, stems removed
    2. 3 cloves garlic, minced
    3. 2 tbsp olive oil
    4. 1 tbsp balsamic vinegar
    5. Salt and pepper to taste

- Instructions:

    1. Preheat the grill or grill pan over medium heat.
    2. In a small bowl, mix olive oil, balsamic vinegar, garlic, salt, and pepper.
    3. Brush the mushrooms with the garlic oil mixture.
    4. Grill for 4-5 minutes on each side until tender.
    5. Serve warm, topped with fresh herbs if desired.

Salmon and Avocado Salad

- Ingredients:

    1. 2 salmon fillets
    2. 1 tbsp olive oil
    3. Salt and pepper to taste
    4. 1 avocado, sliced
    5. 2 cups mixed greens
    6. 1/2 red onion, thinly sliced
    7. 1 tbsp lemon juice

- Instructions:

    1. Preheat the oven to 375°F (190°C). Season the salmon fillets with olive oil, salt, and pepper, and bake for 12-15 minutes, until cooked through.
    2. In a bowl, toss mixed greens, avocado, and red onion.
    3. Top with baked salmon, drizzle with lemon juice, and serve.

Cauliflower Pizza Crust with Veggies

- Ingredients:

    1. 1 small head of cauliflower (or 4 cups cauliflower rice)
    2. 1/2 cup shredded mozzarella cheese
    3. 1/4 cup almond flour
    4. 1 egg
    5. 1 tsp dried oregano
    6. Salt and pepper to taste
    7. Toppings: tomato sauce, fresh veggies, additional cheese

- Instructions:

    1. Preheat the oven to 425°F (220°C). Line a baking sheet with parchment paper.
    2. If using fresh cauliflower, rice it in a food processor. Microwave the cauliflower rice for 5-7 minutes, then let it cool.
    3. Squeeze out excess moisture from the cauliflower using a clean towel.
    4. Mix cauliflower rice with cheese, almond flour, egg, oregano, salt, and pepper to form a dough.
    5. Shape the dough into a pizza crust on the baking sheet and bake for 15-20 minutes, until golden.
    6. Remove from the oven, add desired toppings, and bake for an additional 10 minutes.